I0476617

PIGMENTS OF IMAGINATION

VOL. TWO

PAGES OF CHROMATIC COUTURE

A COLORING BOOK
BY
AMY GRACE SLOAN

Set your creativity free and release the pigments of your imagination as you relax and enjoy these fashionable designs from Rhode Island artist Amy Grace Sloan. Coloring is not just for kids!

You may also enjoy "Pigments of Imagination – Vol. One: Pages for the Prismatic Optimist" and "Art of the Heart: A Human Anatomy Coloring Book for All Ages." And keep an eye out for more coming soon!

PRINTED BY CREATESPACE, AN AMAZON.COM COMPANY

ISBN-13: 978-1514847497
ISBN-10: 1514847493

ENJOY!

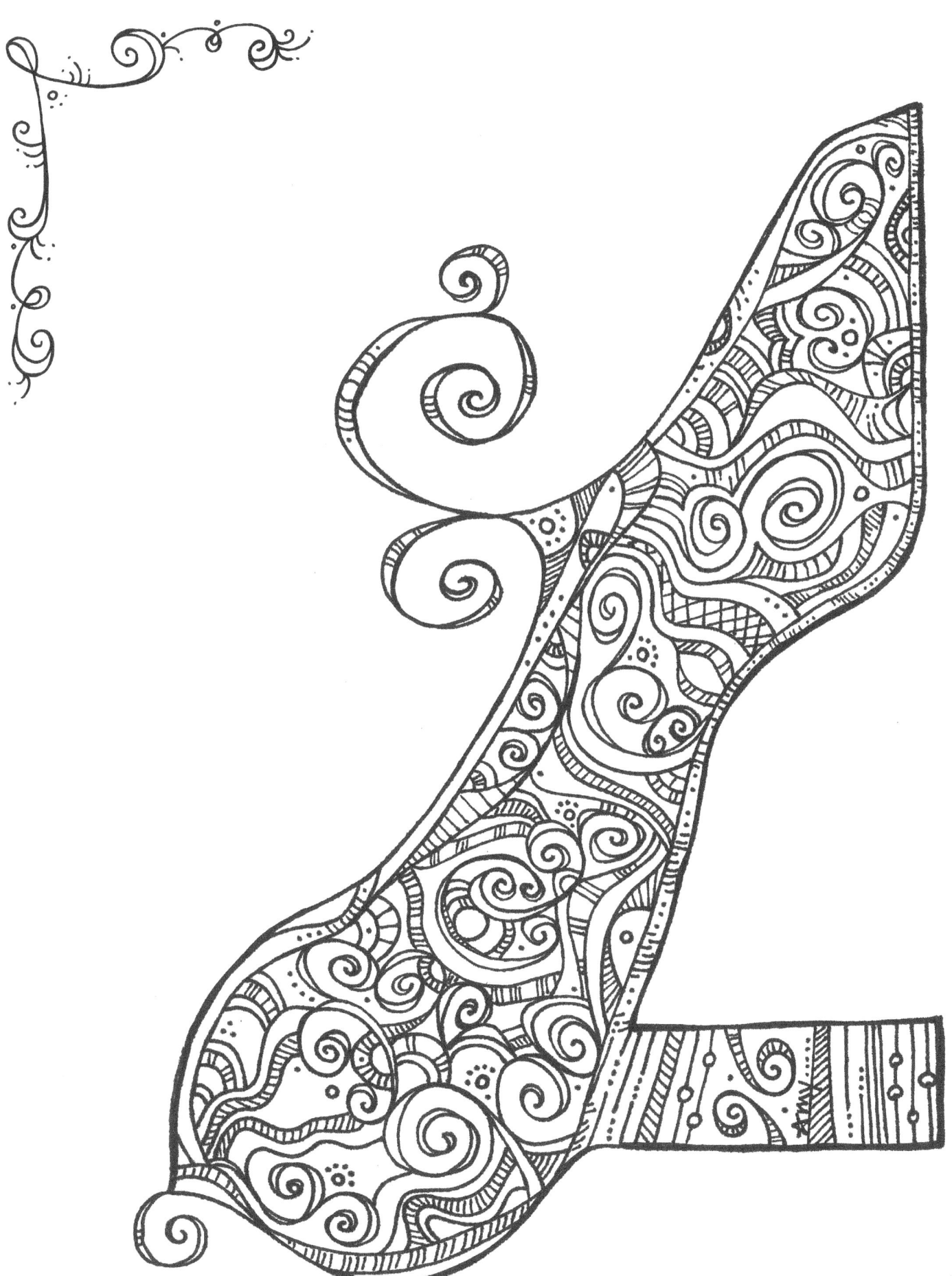

SKETCHES ◆ COLOR TESTS ◆ COLOR CATCHER

SKETCHES ◆ COLOR TESTS ◆ COLOR CATCHER

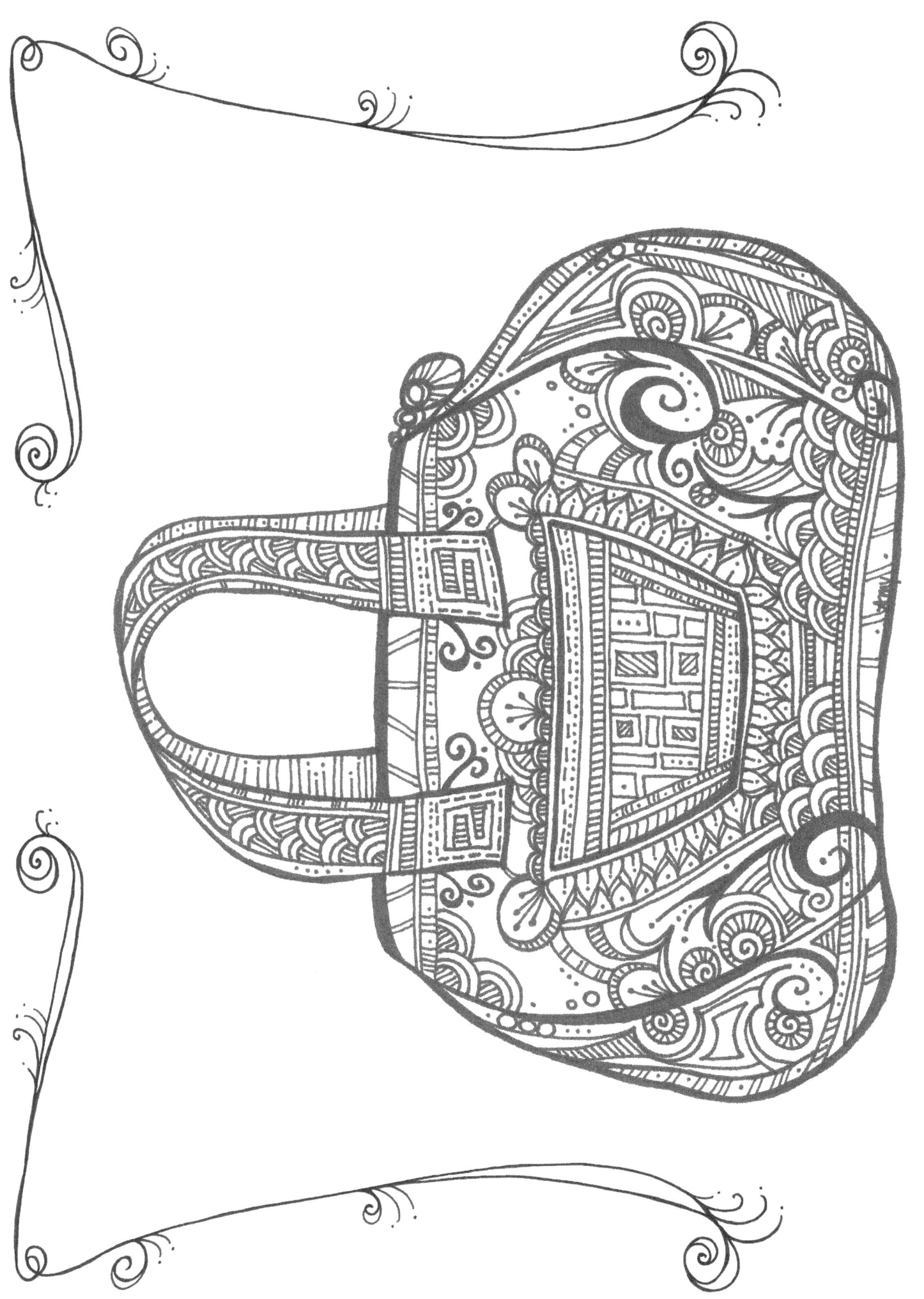

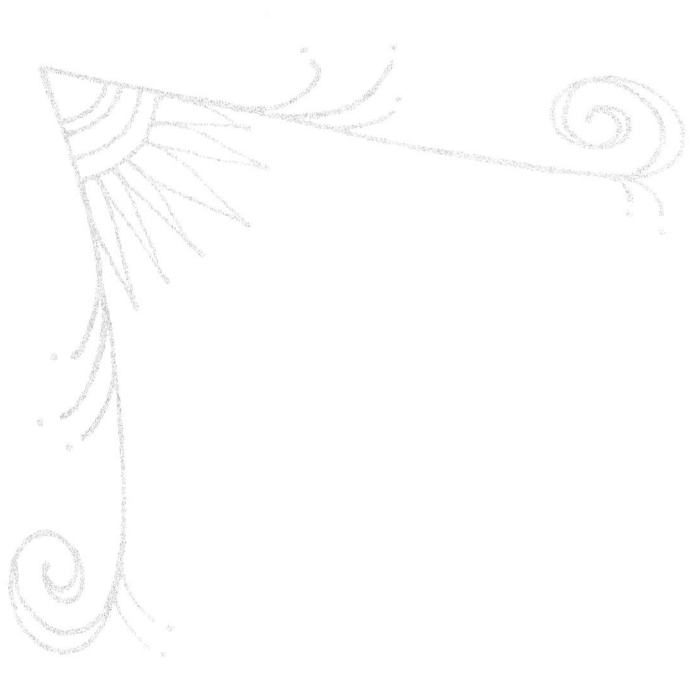

SKETCHES ◆ COLOR TESTS ◆ COLOR CATCHER

SKETCHES ◆ COLOR TESTS ◆ COLOR CATCHER

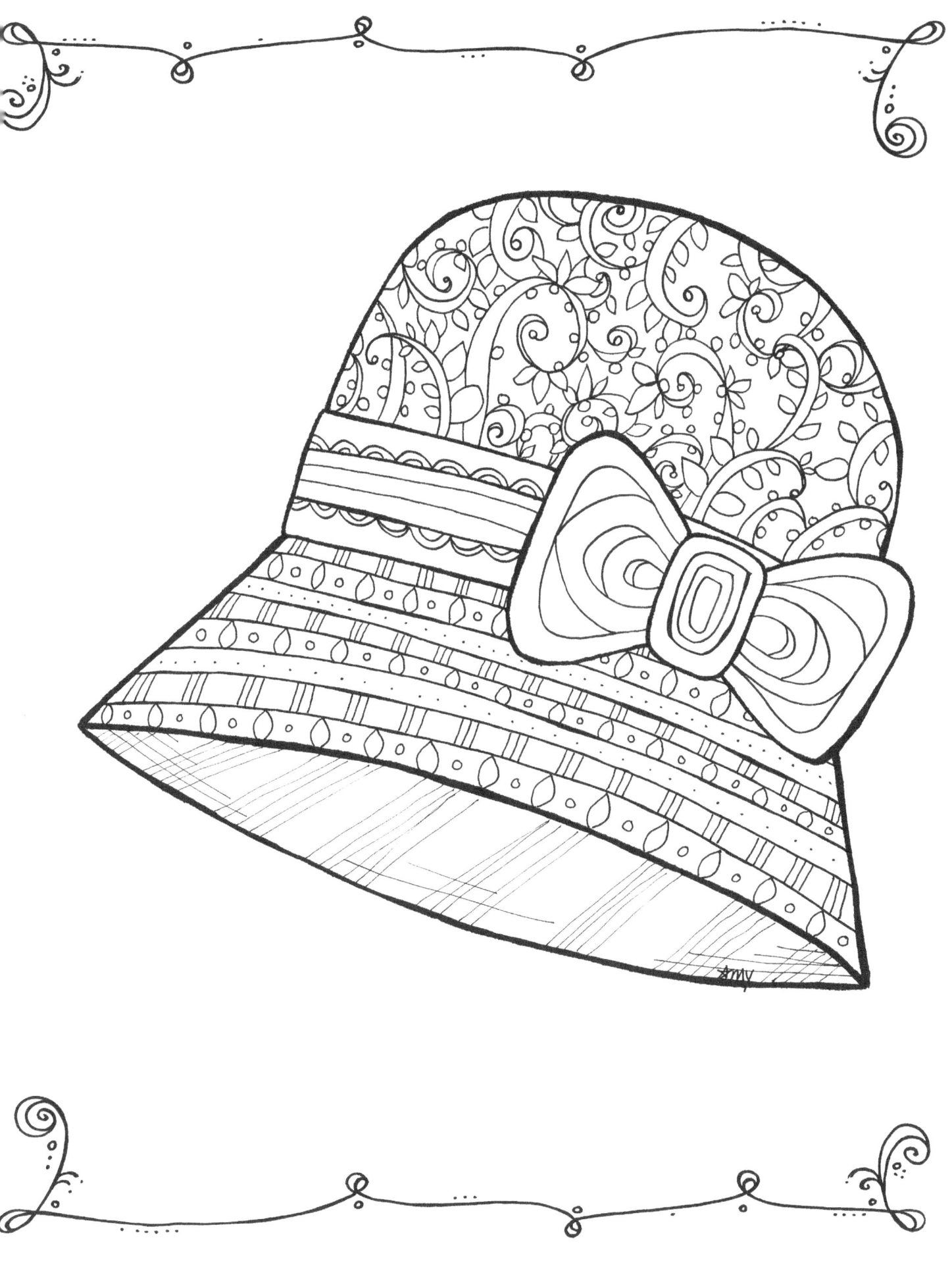

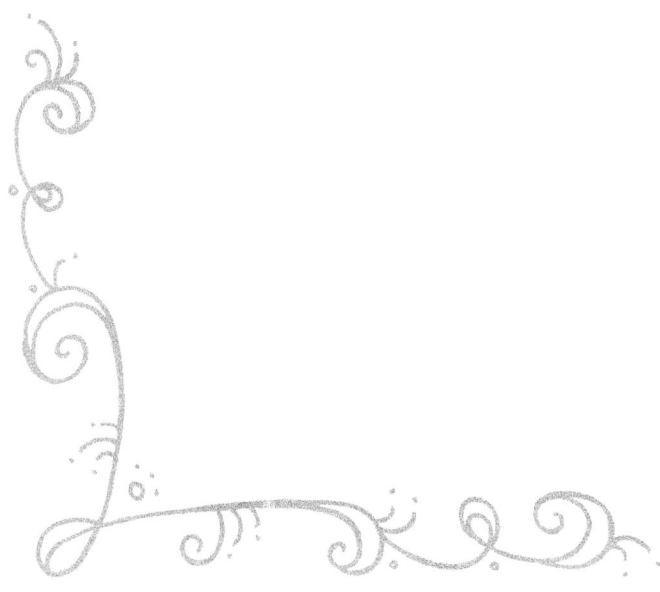

SKETCHES ◆ COLOR TESTS ◆ COLOR CATCHER

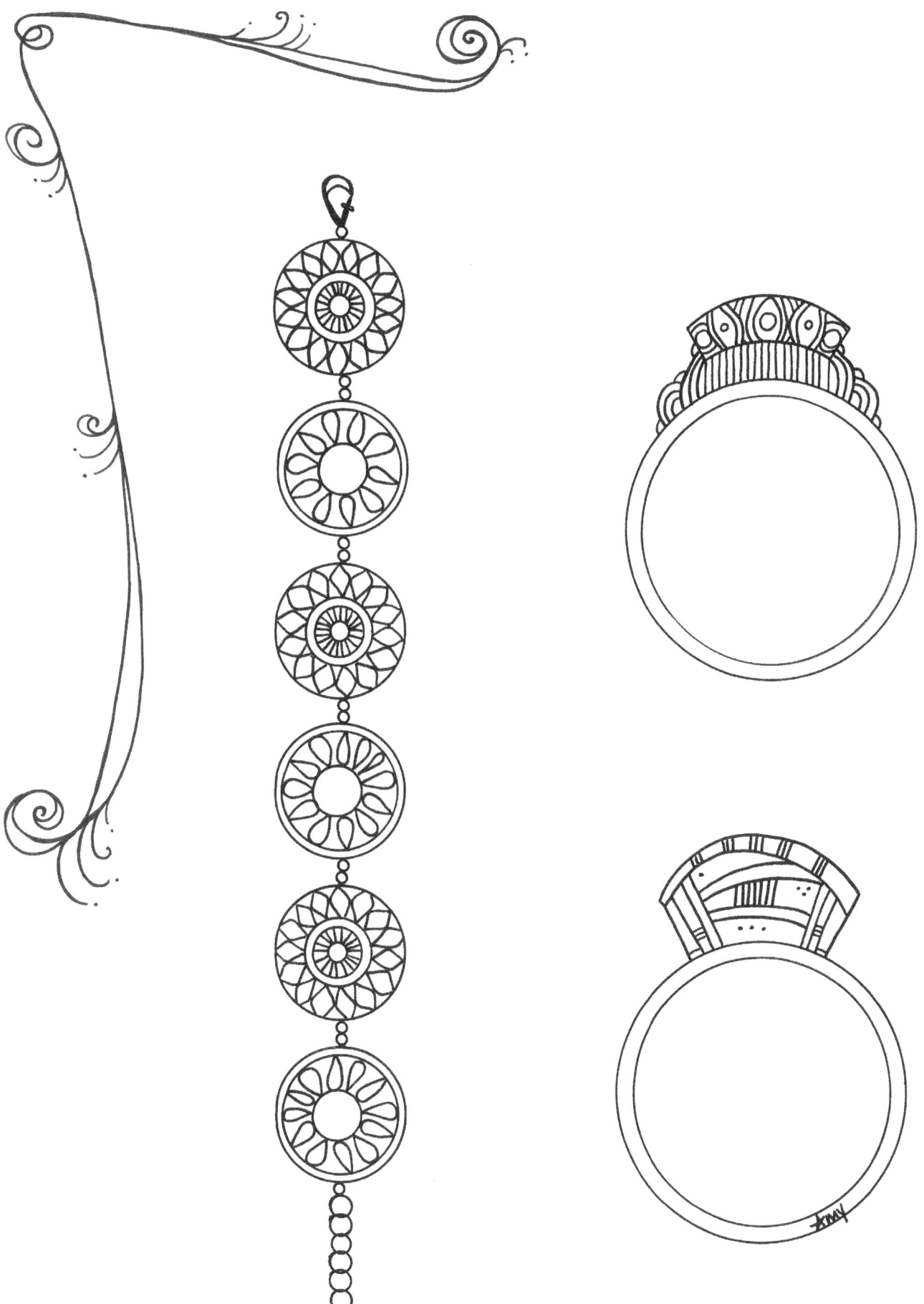

SKETCHES ◆ COLOR TESTS ◆ COLOR CATCHER

SKETCHES ◆ COLOR TESTS ◆ COLOR CATCHER

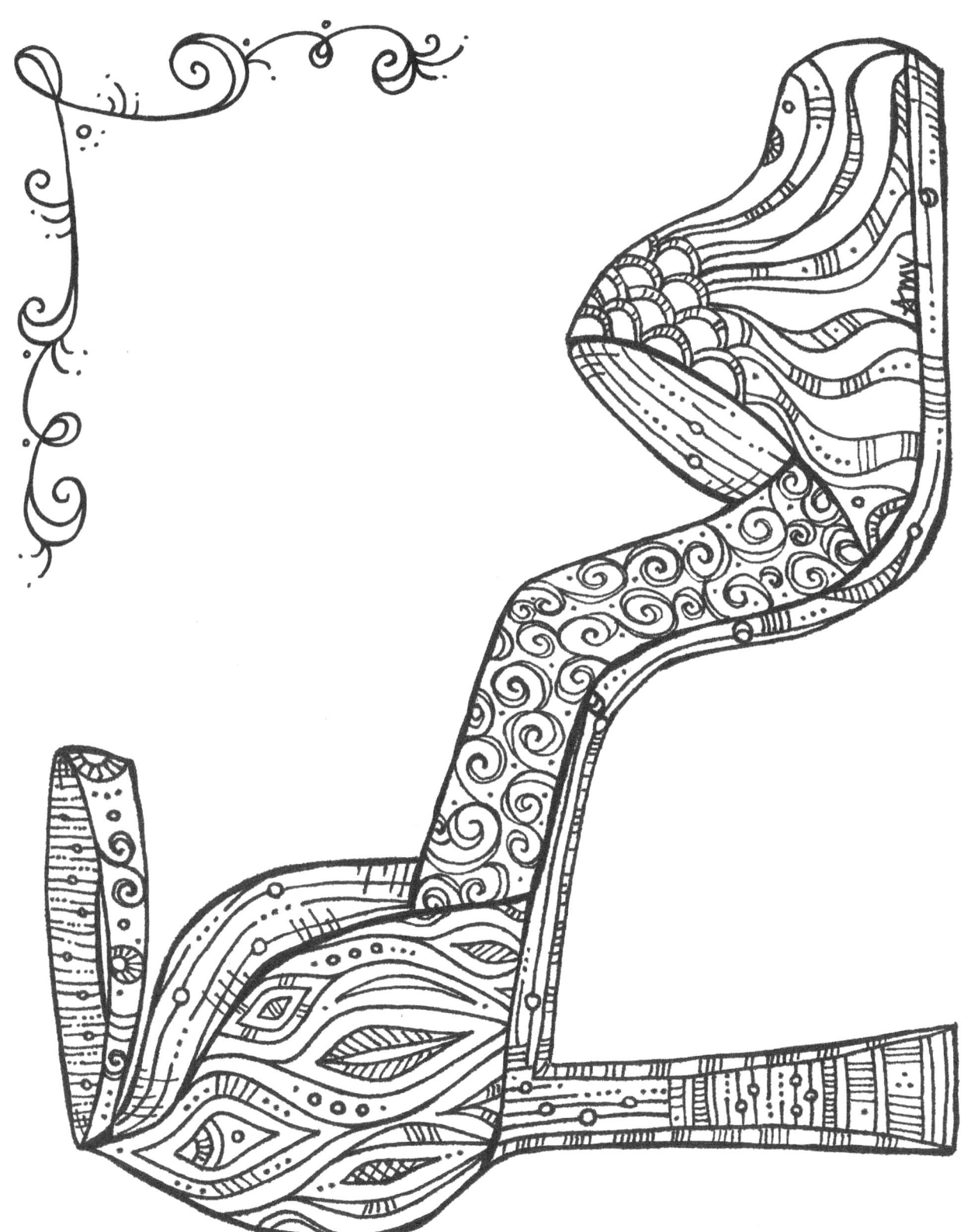

SKETCHES ◆ COLOR TESTS ◆ COLOR CATCHER

SKETCHES ◆ COLOR TESTS ◆ COLOR CATCHER

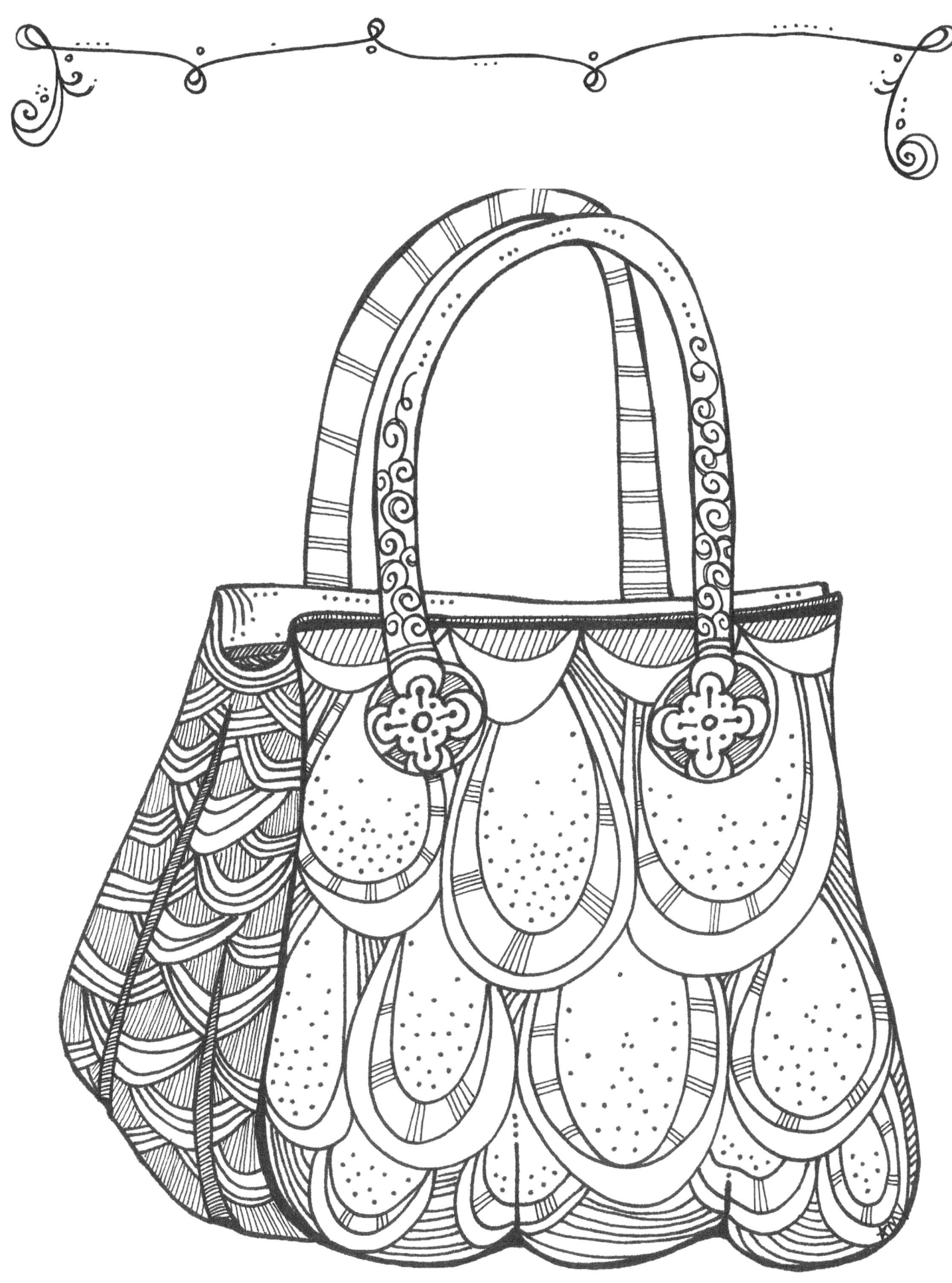

SKETCHES ◆ COLOR TESTS ◆ COLOR CATCHER

SKETCHES ♦ COLOR TESTS ♦ COLOR CATCHER

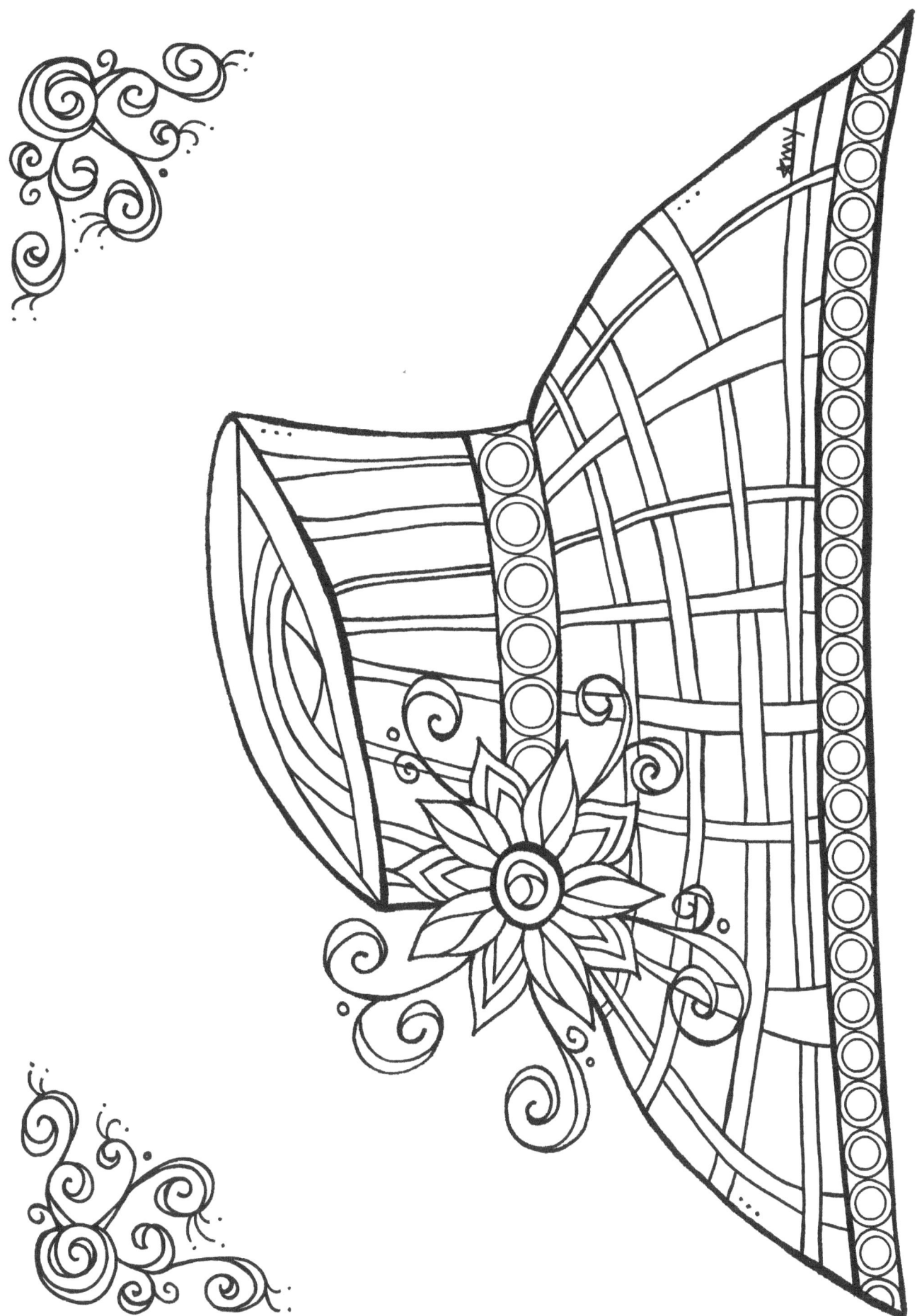

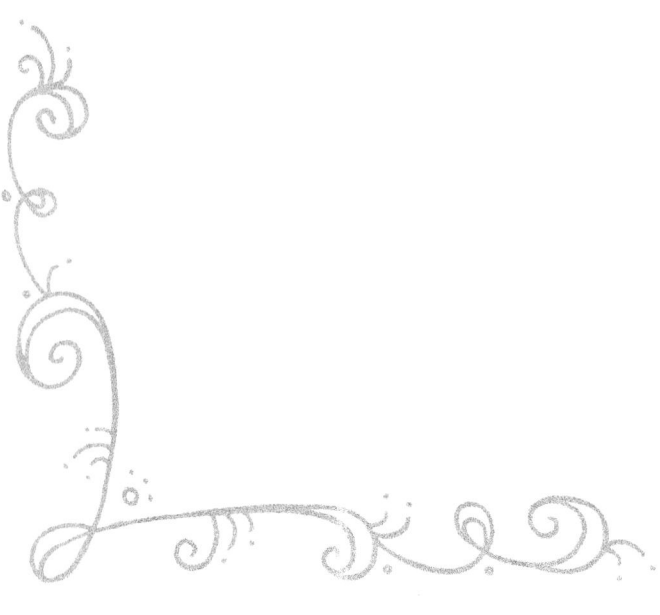

SKETCHES ◆ COLOR TESTS ◆ COLOR CATCHER

SKETCHES ◆ COLOR TESTS ◆ COLOR CATCHER

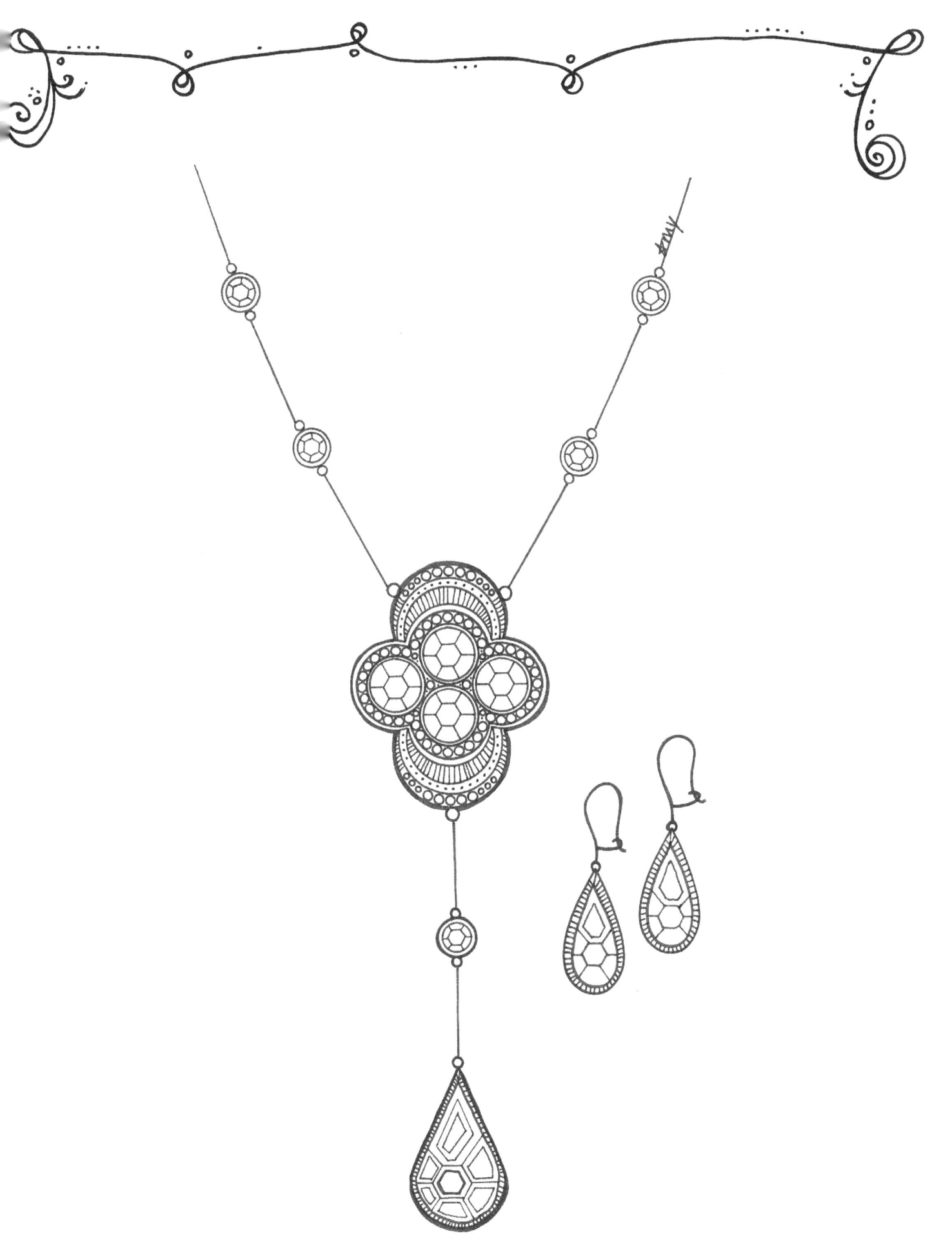

SKETCHES ◆ COLOR TESTS ◆ COLOR CATCHER

SKETCHES ◆ COLOR TESTS ◆ COLOR CATCHER

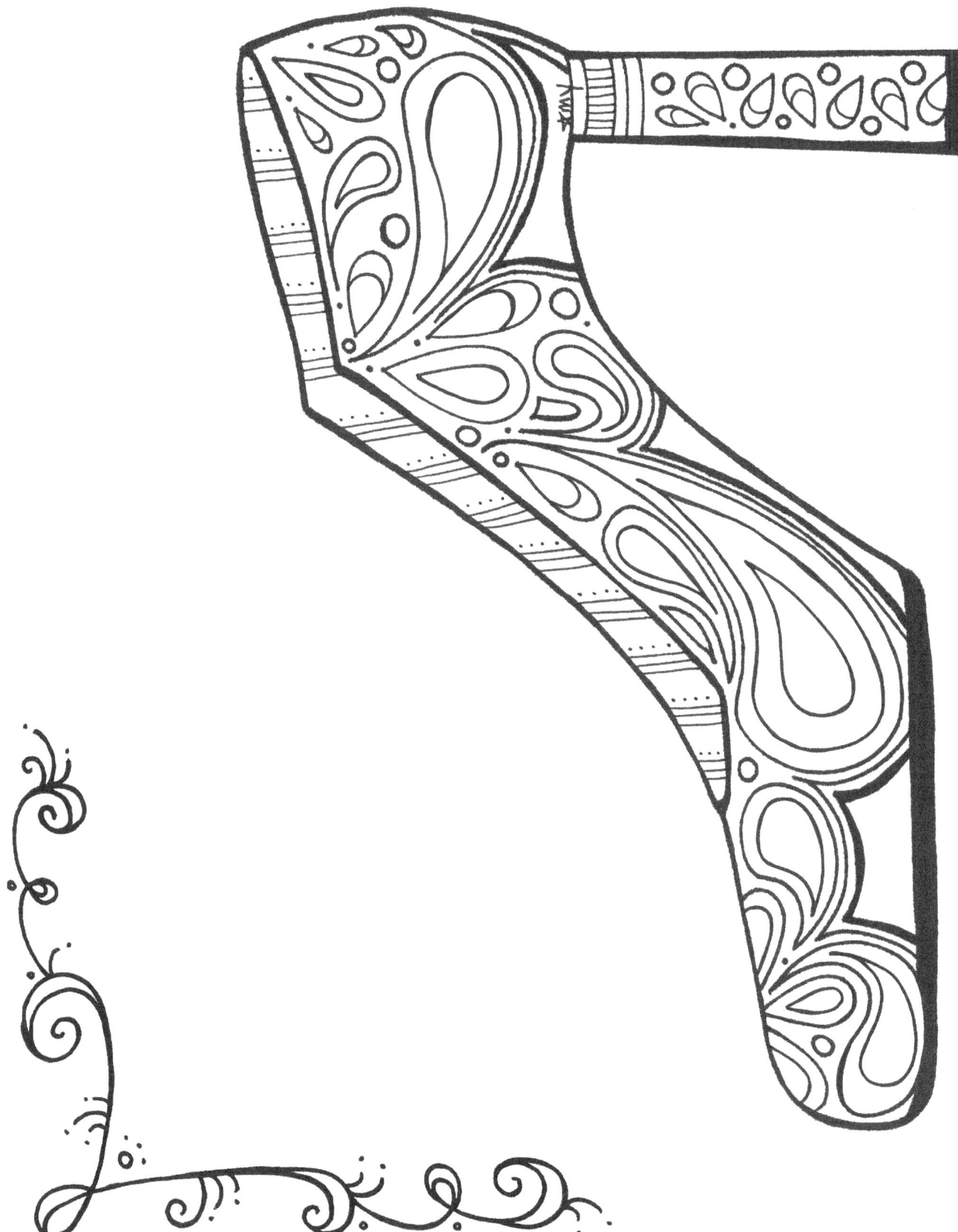

SKETCHES ◆ COLOR TESTS ◆ COLOR CATCHER

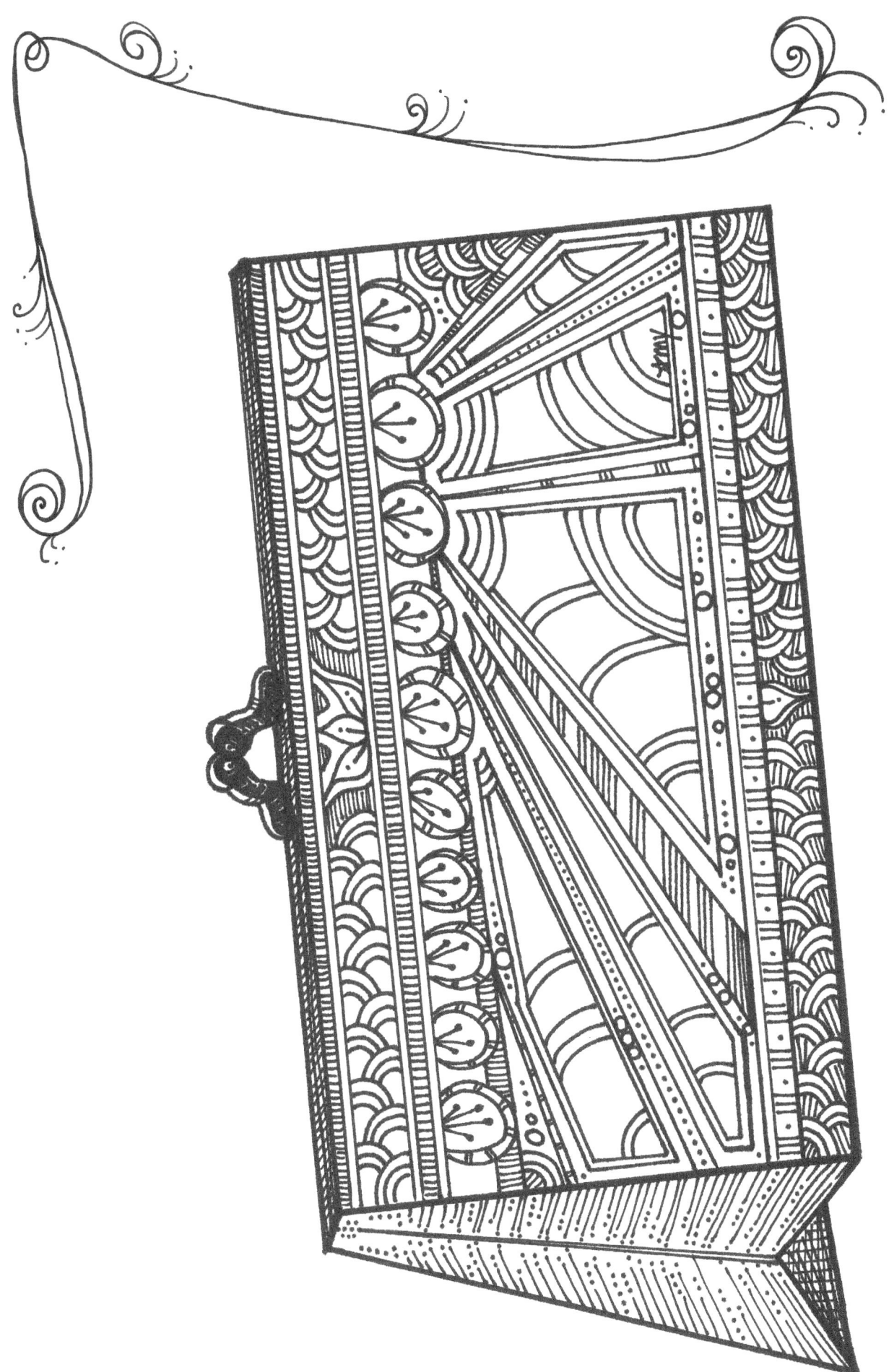

SKETCHES ◆ COLOR TESTS ◆ COLOR CATCHER

SKETCHES ◆ COLOR TESTS ◆ COLOR CATCHER

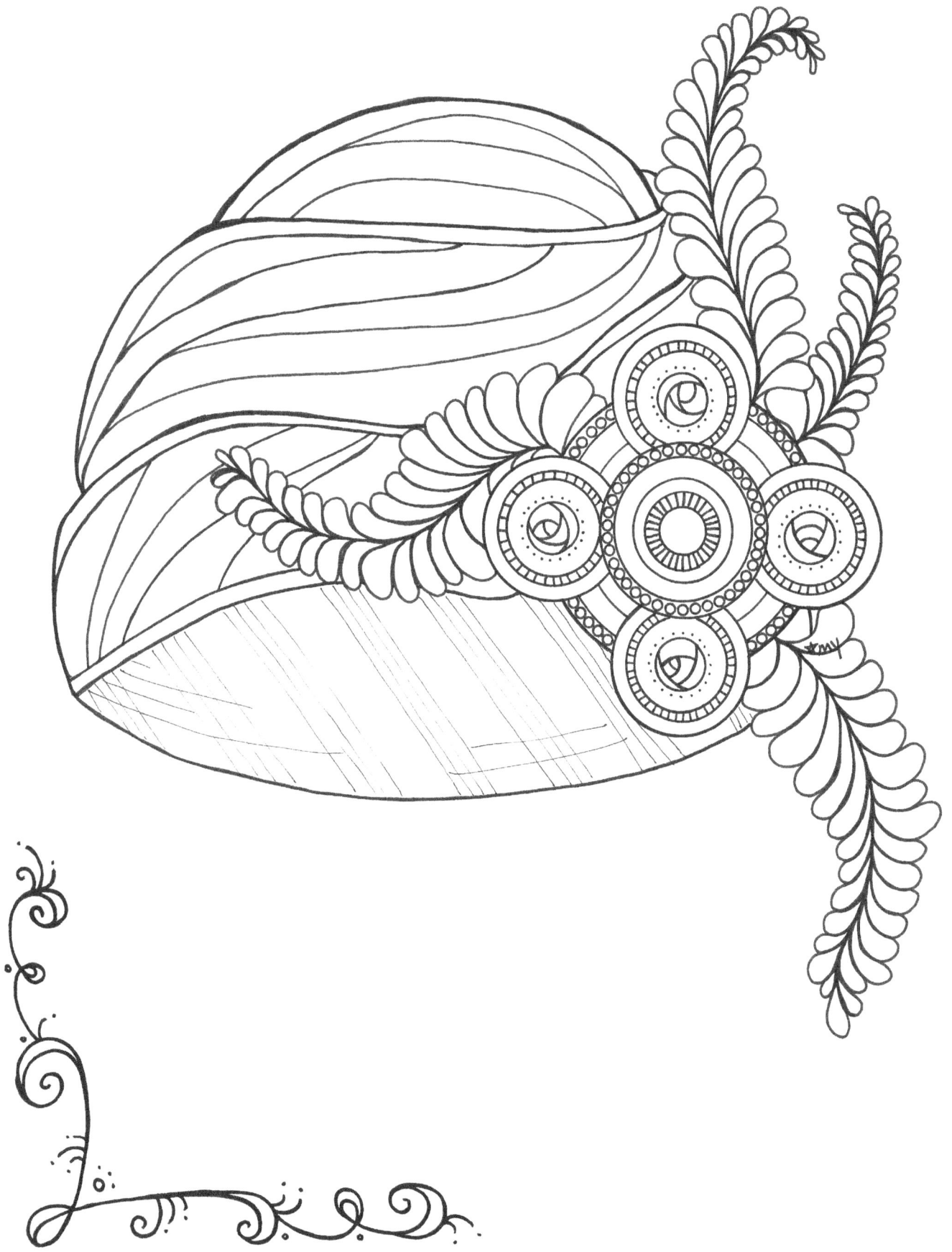

SKETCHES ◆ COLOR TESTS ◆ COLOR CATCHER

SKETCHES ◆ COLOR TESTS ◆ COLOR CATCHER

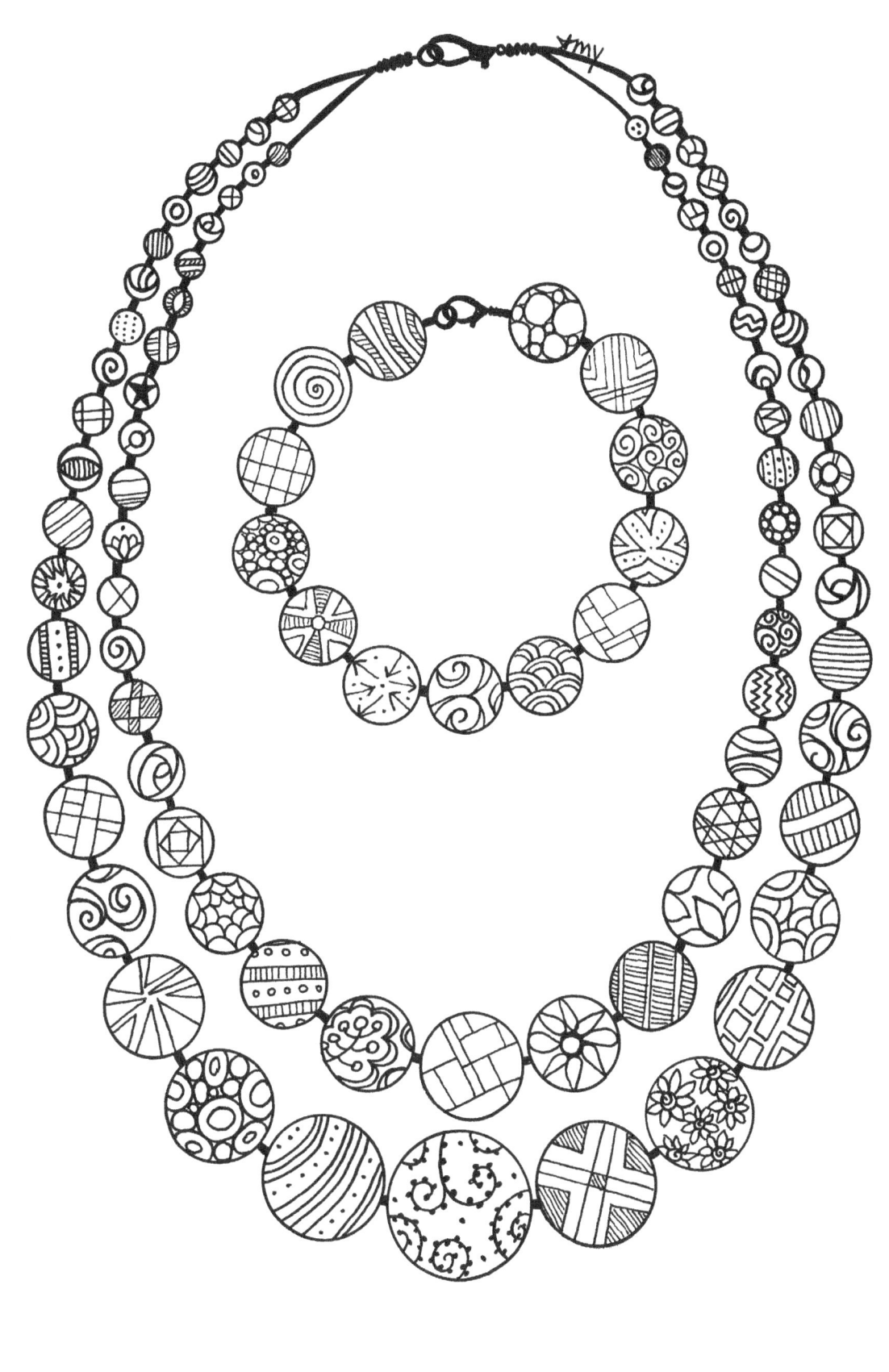

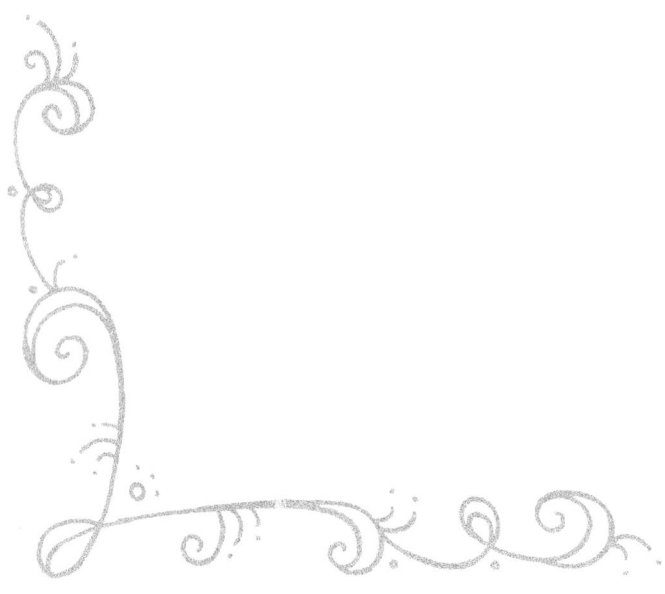

SKETCHES ◆ COLOR TESTS ◆ COLOR CATCHER

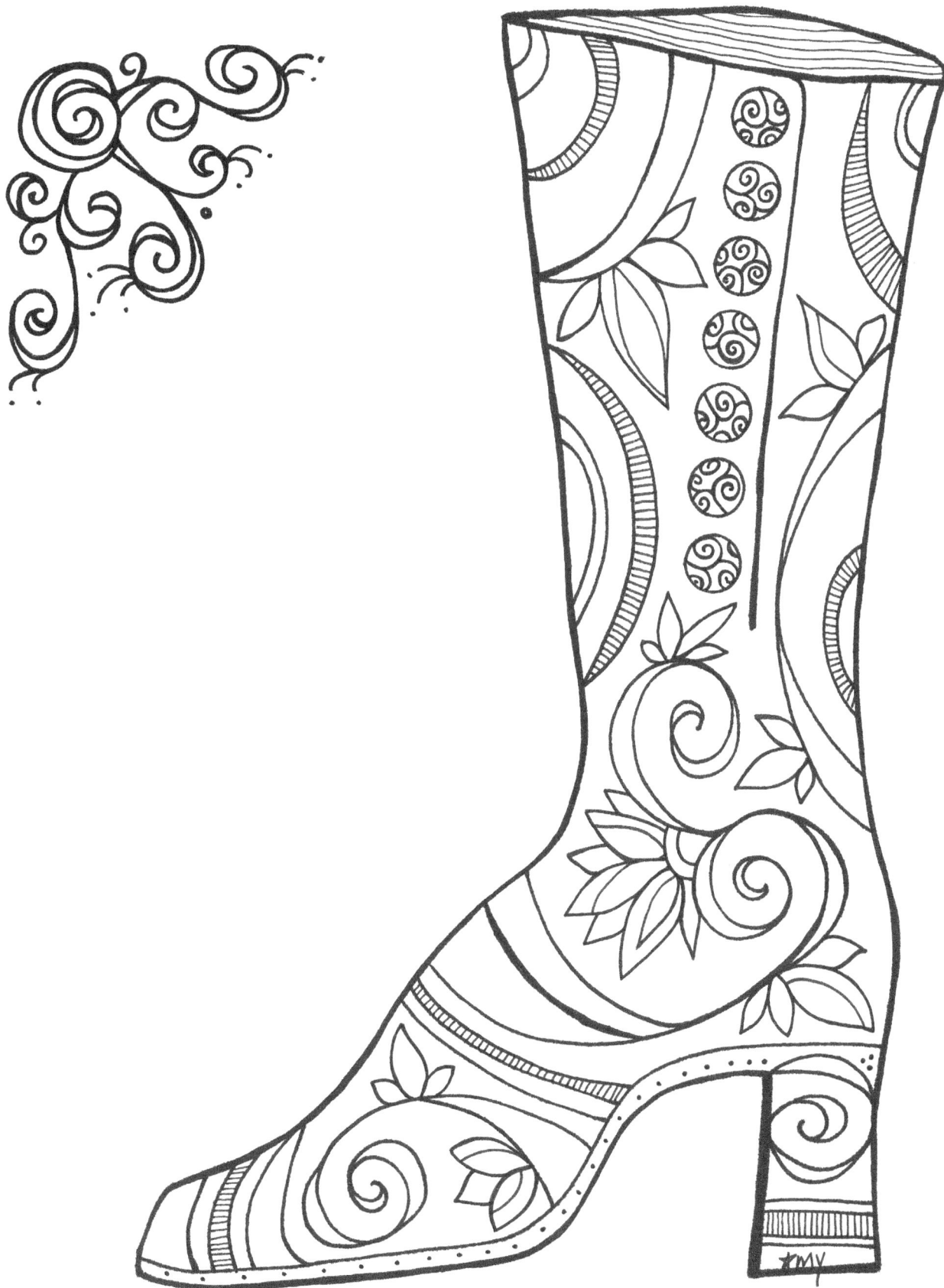

SKETCHES ◆ COLOR TESTS ◆ COLOR CATCHER

SKETCHES ◆ COLOR TESTS ◆ COLOR CATCHER

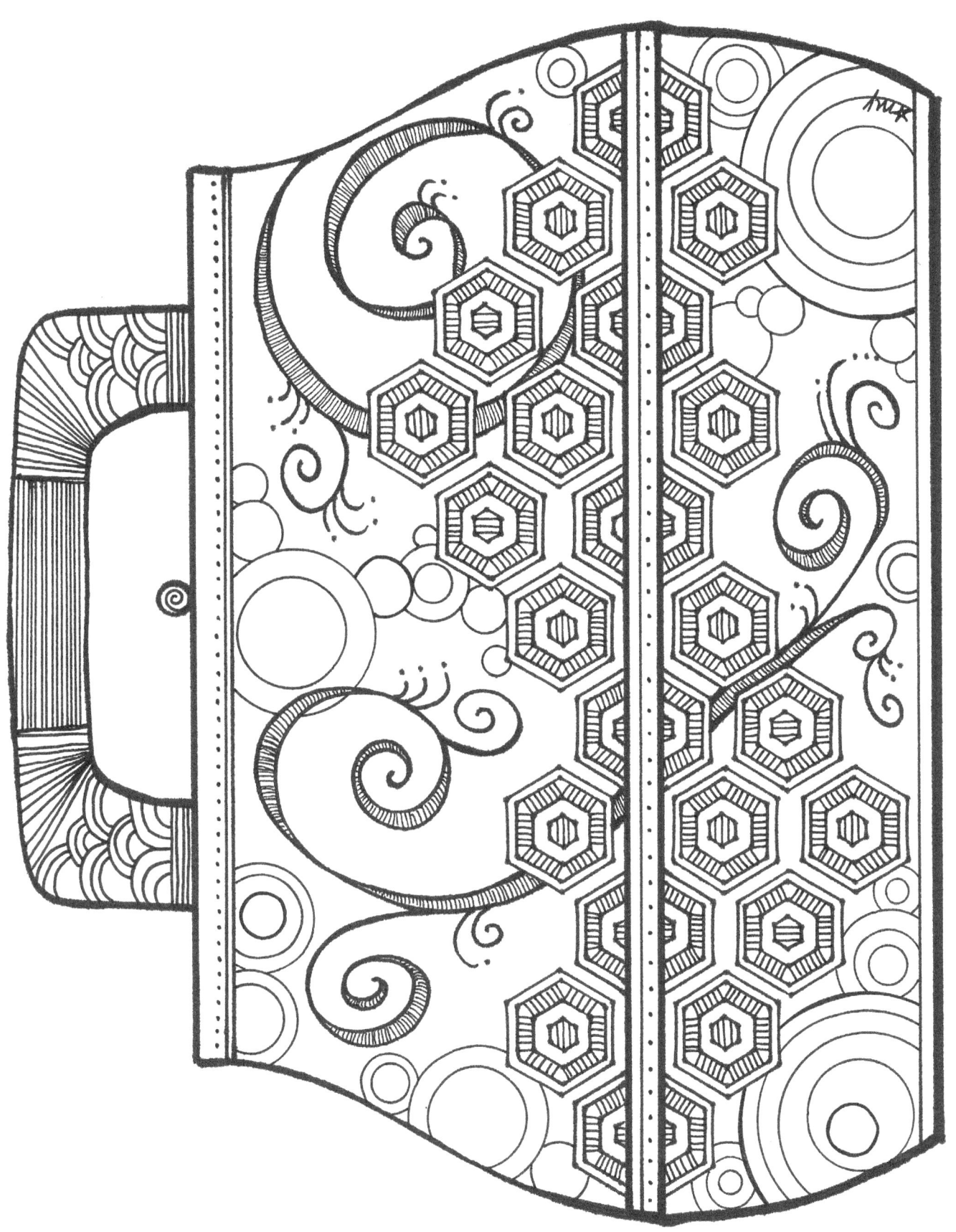

SKETCHES ◆ COLOR TESTS ◆ COLOR CATCHER

SKETCHES ◆ COLOR TESTS ◆ COLOR CATCHER

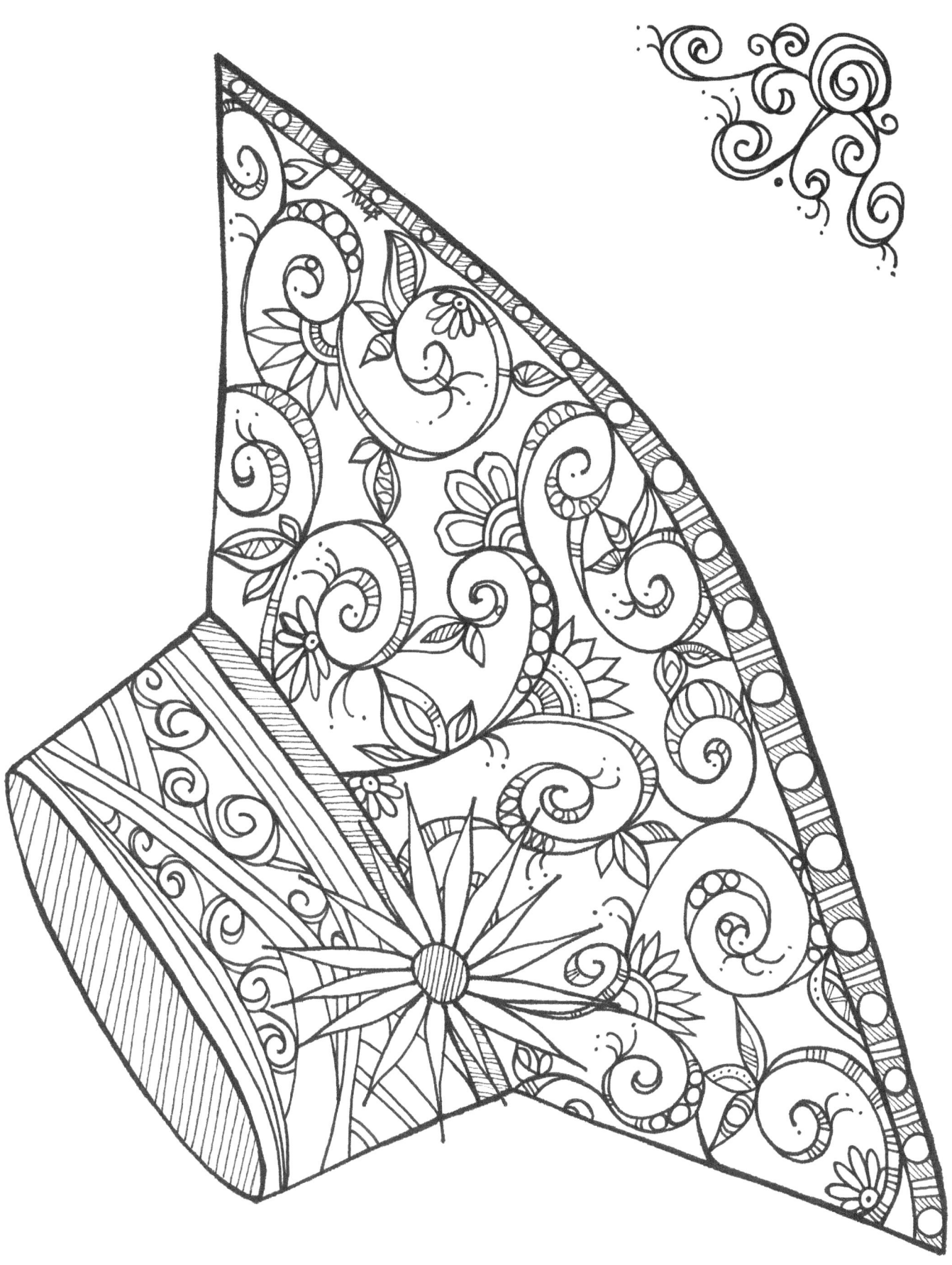

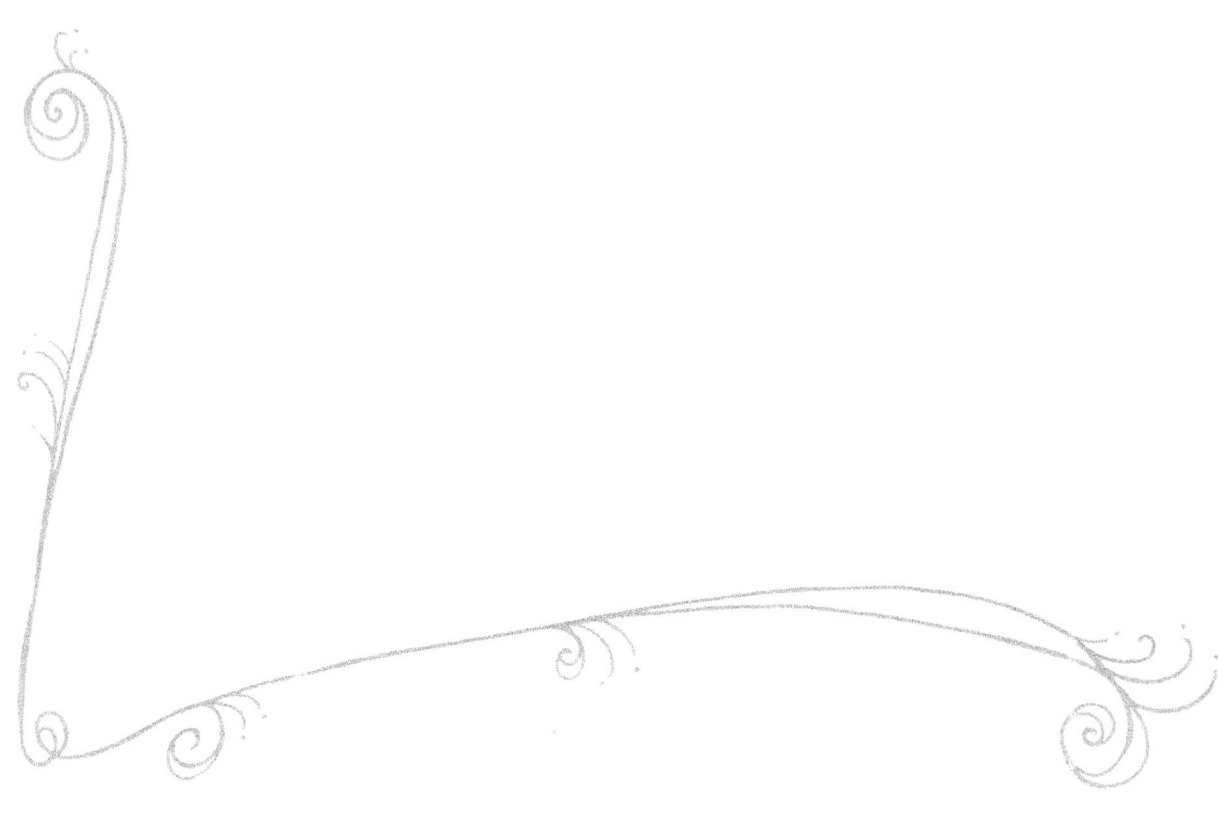

SKETCHES ◆ COLOR TESTS ◆ COLOR CATCHER

SKETCHES ◆ COLOR TESTS ◆ COLOR CATCHER

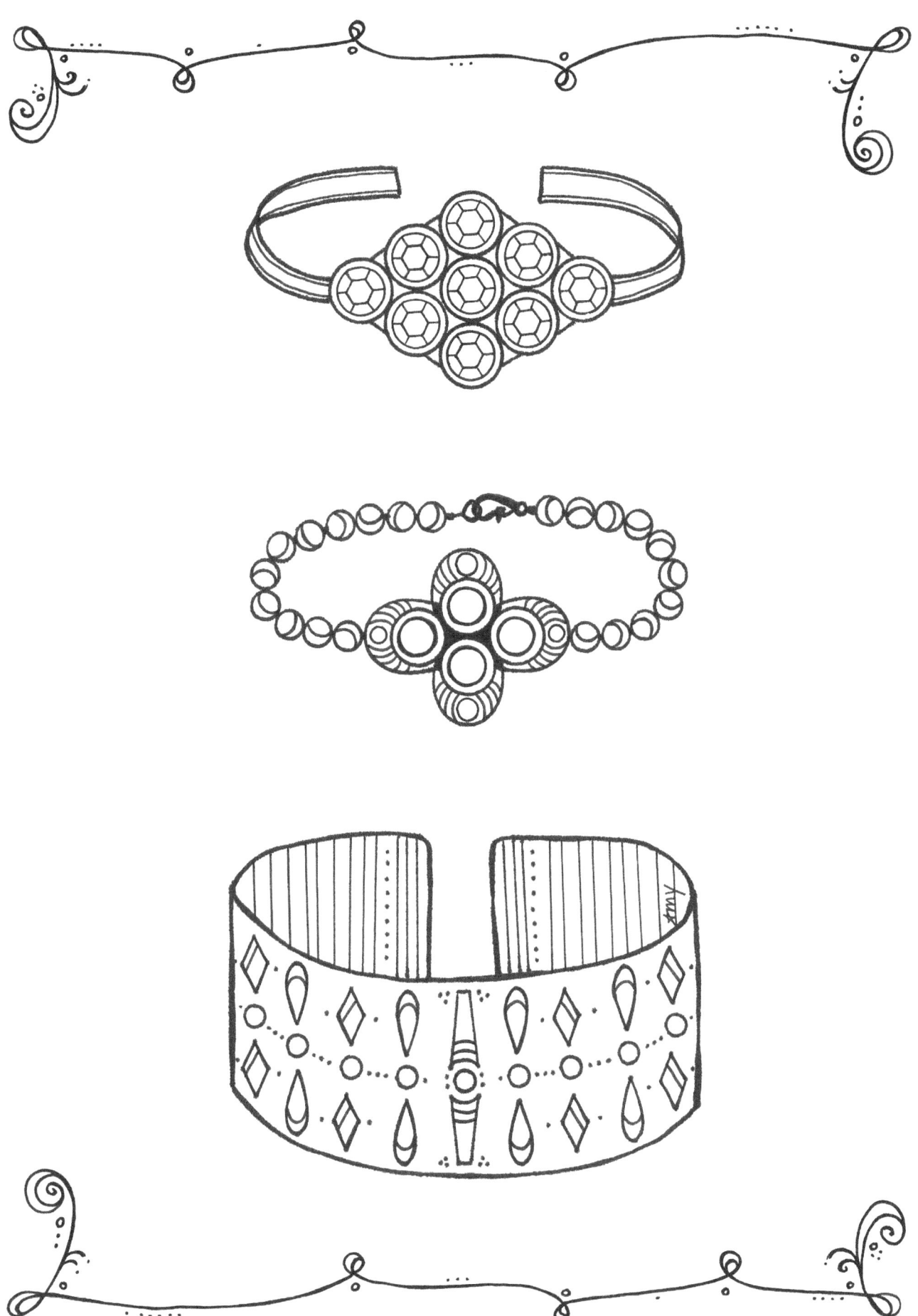

SKETCHES ◆ COLOR TESTS ◆ COLOR CATCHER

SKETCHES ◆ COLOR TESTS ◆ COLOR CATCHER

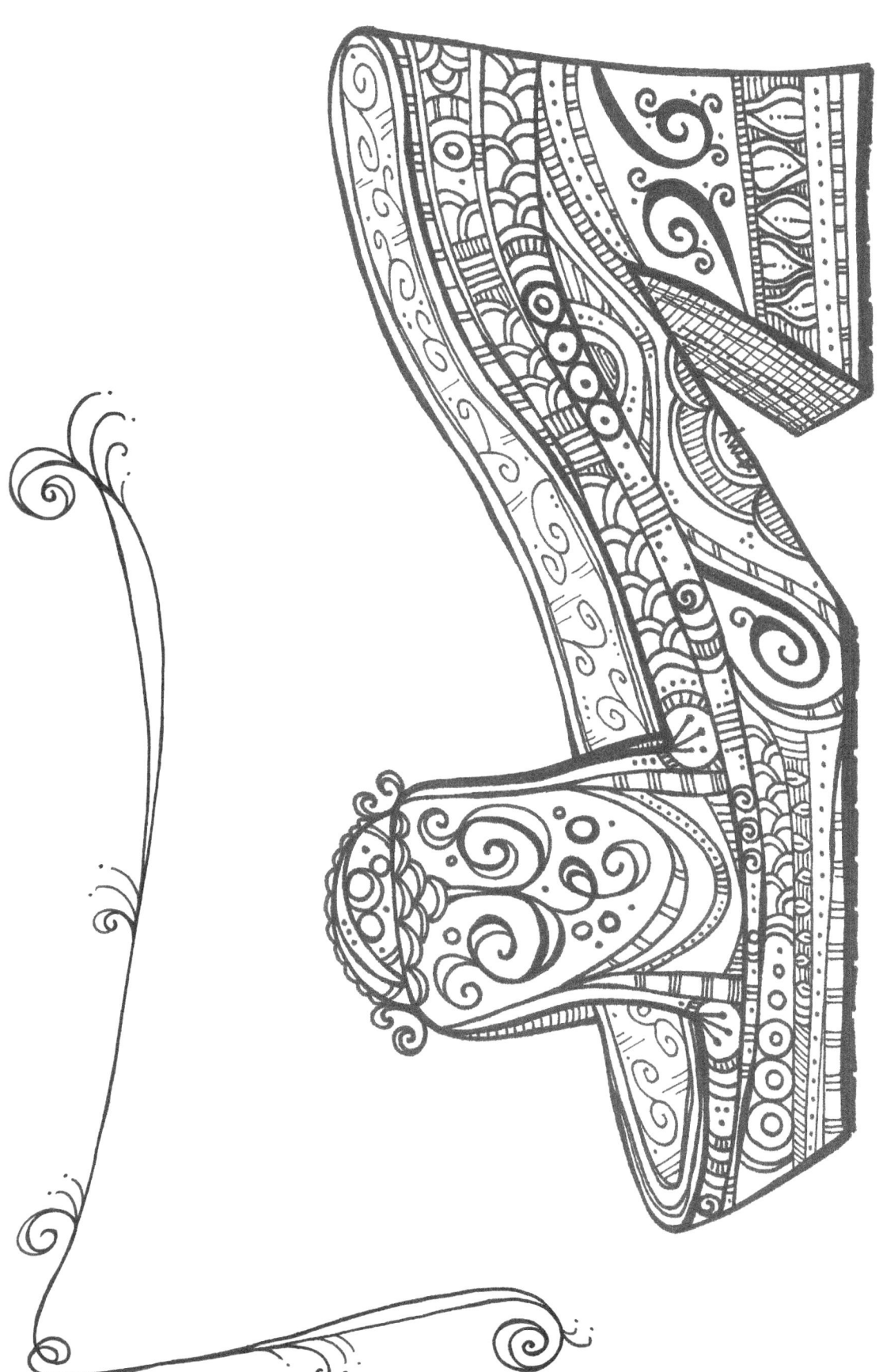

SKETCHES ◆ COLOR TESTS ◆ COLOR CATCHER

SKETCHES ◆ COLOR TESTS ◆ COLOR CATCHER

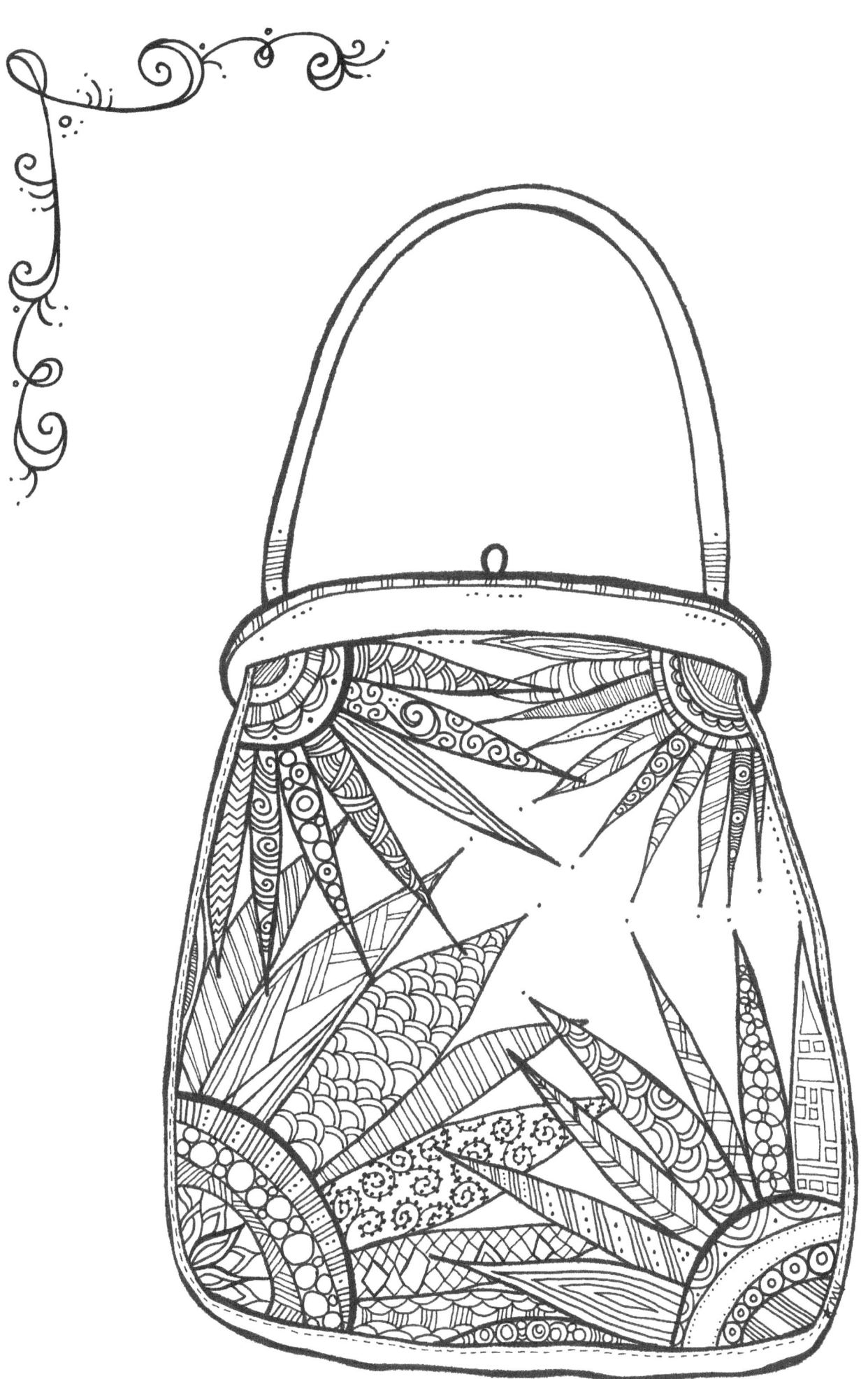